OUR PRESIDENTS
THEIR LIVES AND STORIES

In the 215 years since George Washington's inauguration, many individuals have aspired to become president. A select few have achieved this goal. *Our Presidents: Their Lives and Stories* chronicles these leaders' paths to the presidency, the events that defined their terms, and the activities that they pursued after leaving office. Each entry includes photos or paintings of the president and an excerpt from a speech.

ideals

Digging Up Dinosaurs

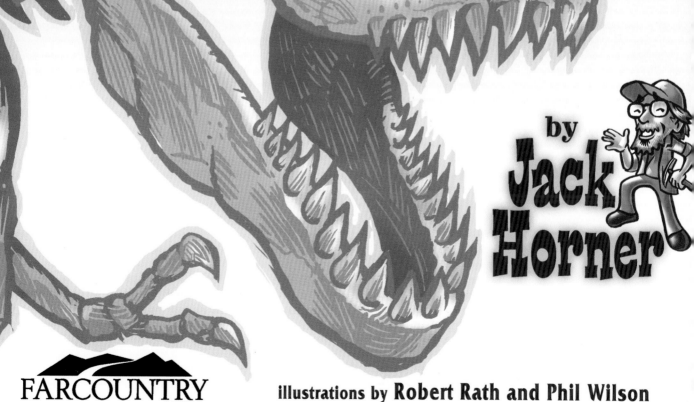

by **Jack Horner**

FARCOUNTRY PRESS

illustrations by **Robert Rath** and **Phil Wilson**

Credits

Robert Rath, www.robertrath.net: cover; back cover; borders (sky, land, tree); page 1 (all); page 4 (map); page 5 (all); page 7 (Jack); page 9 (all); page 10 (headstone); page 11-12 (all); page 14 (Jack); page 15 (all); page 17 (all); page 18 (map); page 19 (all); page 20 (all); page 22-23 (all); page 25 (dino); page 27 (helicopter, Jack); page 28 (all); page 29 (Jack, plant); page 32 (all); page 33 (Jack); page 34 (tracks); page 35 (Jack); page 36 (all); page 37 (bone); page 39 (Jack); page 40 (all); page 41 (all); page 42 (Jack); page 44 (map background); page 47 (Jack); page 48 (all)

Phil Wilson: page 3 (background); page 8 (coelurosaur); page 9 (background); page 10 (T. rex); page 11 (all); page 30-31 (background); page 33 (triceratops); page 34 (brachiosaurus herd); page 38–39 (background); page 42 (background); page 44-45 (dinosaurs); page 46 (Stegosaurus)

Jack Horner: photos, pages 6, 14, 16 (hadrosaur bone, duckbill eggs), 20, 21, 24, 25, 26, 27, 29, 30, 31, 33, 35, 37, 38

Mary Schweitzer: page 39 (blood vessels)

Monte Dolack, www.dolack.com: page 43 (Maiasaura)

The Field Museum of Chicago: #GN89671_53c, page 39 (Sue)

Royal Saskatchewan Museum: page 16 (coprolite)

Helena Independent Record: back cover (author photo); photos, page 5, 18

ISBN 10: 1-56037-396-2
ISBN 13: 978-1-56037-396-4

For more information on our books, write Farcountry Press, P.O. Box 5630, Helena, MT 59604; call (800) 821-3874; or visit www.farcountrypress.com.

Library of Congress Cataloging-in-Publication Data

Horner, John R.
  Digging up dinosaurs with Jack Horner / by Jack Horner.
    p. cm.
  ISBN-13: 978-1-56037-396-4
  ISBN-10: 1-56037-396-2
  1. Paleontology--Rocky Mountains--Juvenile literature. 2. Dinosaurs--Rocky Mountains--Juvenile literature. I. Title.

  QE714.5.H67 2007
  567.9--dc22
                                          2006014537

Created, produced, and designed in the United States.
Printed in China.

12 11 10 09 08 07   1 2 3 4 5 6

Contents

Dinosaurs lived everywhere on Earth. But some of the most important dinosaur fossil finds have been in the Rocky Mountain and Badland regions.

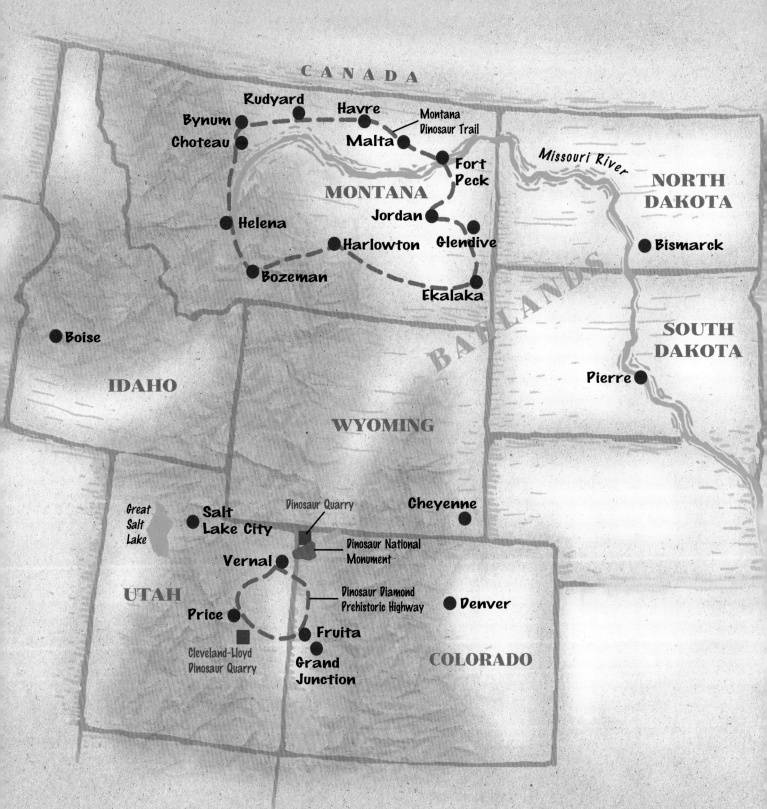

Meet Paleontologist Jack Horner

Hi! I'm Jack Horner. I've got the best job in the world! I'm a paleontologist. A dinosaur paleontologist!

A **PALEONTOLOGIST** (PAY-lee-uhn-TAHL-uh-jihst) is a person who studies fossils to learn about ancient animals and plants.

FOSSILS are the mineralized remains (such as bone) and traces (such as footprints) of these ancient animals and plants.

Dinosaur Detectives

I'm like a dinosaur detective. My job is to find dinosaur skeletons and study how the animals looked and behaved when they were alive.

I've found hundreds of dinosaur skeletons, some of which were species that no one had ever found before. I even got to name them! I'll tell you about that later in the book!

STAY TUNED!

The word *fossil* comes from the Latin word *fossus*, which means "dug up."

Hadrosaur bone fossil created by permineralization

Wood fossil created by petrification

Petri-what?

Here are a couple of big words that every young paleontologist should know: petrification and permineralization. These are the two ways that fossils are formed!

Petrified wood is a type of fossil formed by **petrification** *(PEH-trih-fih-KAY-shun)*. The organic material (carbon) in the wood is replaced with minerals (usually silica) and retains the original structure of the wood. Petrification takes place in plants (under the right conditions) and rarely occurs in animal bones.

Permineralization *(per-MIN-er-uhl-ih-ZAY-shun)* is what happens to some animal bones after the animal dies and becomes buried by mineral-rich groundwater. The bone material *remains,* and the spaces in the bones are filled in with minerals. Permineralization can occur in plants, too, and it produces very detailed fossils.

JUST THE FACTS!

Although fossil bones look like rocks, they aren't. They are still bone. Over time, minerals have filled in the spaces in the bone where the vessels, nerves, and marrow were when the dinosaur was alive. The original bone is still there. Fossil bones are heavy because they are filled with minerals.

What Were the Dinosaurs?

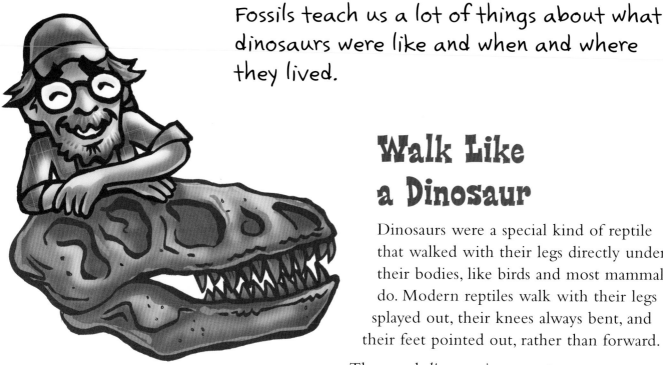

Fossils teach us a lot of things about what dinosaurs were like and when and where they lived.

Walk Like a Dinosaur

Dinosaurs were a special kind of reptile that walked with their legs directly under their bodies, like birds and most mammals do. Modern reptiles walk with their legs splayed out, their knees always bent, and their feet pointed out, rather than forward.

The word *dinosaur* is Greek for "terrible lizard." But dinosaurs weren't really lizards—they were reptiles—and they weren't necessarily terrible.

DID YOU KNOW?

Dinosaurs were sometimes very large and sometimes quite small. Some were CARNIVORES (CAR-nih-vorz), which means they ate other animals. Others were HERBIVORES (ERB-ih-vorz) and ate plants. Some dinosaurs may have been OMNIVORES (AHM-nih-vorz), which means they ate both plants and other animals.

The Age of the Dinosaurs

Dinosaurs roamed the Earth from 240 million years ago until 65 million years ago. (None of the dinosaurs actually lived that long.) This period of time is called the **Mesozoic** *(MES-oh-ZOH-ick)* **Era.**

Cenozoic Era
65 million years ago to today

Mesozoic Era
240 million years ago to 65 million years ago

Paleozoic Era
544 million years ago to 240 million years ago

Proterozoic Era
2,500 million years ago to 544 million years ago

Dawn of Time
137,000 million years ago

Living Dinosaurs

Although dinosaurs are now extinct, their descendents walk the Earth today. Believe it or not, their relatives are birds!

Some people think that birds evolved from all dinosaurs, including the **TYRANNOSAURUS REX** *(tih-RAN-uh-SAWR-us reks)*. This is not true. Birds evolved from one group of small meat-eating dinosaurs called **COELUROSAURS** *(see-LOOR-oh-sawrz)*. They had hollow bones and three-toed feet like birds. And some had feathers just like birds, too!

hollow bones

three-toed feet

Coelurosaur

JUST THE FACTS!

Most people who study dinosaurs consider birds to be dinosaurs. We refer to traditional, extinct dinosaurs as NON-AVIAN DINOSAURS. And we refer to birds as AVIAN DINOSAURS.

Wooly mammoth

Mosasaur

Saber-toothed tiger

Not a Dinosaur

Now extinct, **SABER-TOOTHED TIGERS,
WOOLY MAMMOTHS,** and reptiles such
as **MOSASAURS** *(MOH-zuh-sawrz)* and
PLESIOSAURS *(PLEE-see-oh-sawrz)*
were *not dinosaurs.* Dinosaurs
only include the reptiles
that walked with their
legs directly under
their bodies, and not
sprawled like reptiles
we see today.

Plesiosaur

Extinction Mystery

When dinosaurs went extinct about 65 million years ago, it marked the end of the non-avian dinosaurs—only the avian dinosaurs survived.

Tyrannosaurus with flock of Nyctosaurus

What caused the extinction is a mystery, but some paleontologists think that a meteor crashed into the Earth on the coast of Mexico. An impact like that would have blasted tons of water, dirt, rocks, and plant matter into the upper atmosphere, where the debris formed clouds and blocked out the sun. In the darkness the trees and plants would have died. Because the plant-eating dinosaurs wouldn't have anything to eat, they would have died, and then the meat-eaters followed.

EVOLUTION AND EXTINCTION

Dinosaurs, like all other animals and plants, EVOLVED (changed) and went EXTINCT (died out) over time. Evolution and extinction are the reasons why we have so many different kinds of fossil animals in the fossil record. Evolution and extinction have been taking place on Earth for more than three billion years!

What Do You Think?

A meteor may explain what happened to the non-avian dinosaurs, but what about the avian dinosaurs? Why didn't birds become extinct? Nobody can explain why the big, clunky dinosaurs went extinct but not the birds. The meteor idea might be right, but it's probably not the whole answer.

Maybe one day you can figure out this mystery.

DINO-STATS
OF THE ROCKIES AND BADLANDS

LARGEST: Brachiosaurus (BRACK-ee-oh-SAWR-us), 80 feet long, 40 feet tall

SMALLEST: Orodromeus (OR-oh-DROHM-ee-us), 6 feet long, 2 feet tall

FASTEST: Troodon (TROH-oh-don), 20 miles an hour

Brachiosaurus

Orodromeus

Troodon

MESOZOIC ERA
IN THE ROCKY MOUNTAINS AND BADLANDS

TRIASSIC PERIOD

240 million years ago to 200 million years ago

When: JURASSIC PERIOD, 200 million years ago to 145 million years ago

Where: Montana, Idaho, Wyoming, North and South Dakota, Utah, and Colorado

What: The continent of Pangaea began to separate. The Atlantic Ocean formed as the continents of Africa and North America pulled apart. A great coastal plain spread across eastern Montana and North and South Dakota. Dinosaurs lived alongside streams in Colorado, Utah, and Wyoming.

Who: Allosaurus, Brachiosaurus, Diplodocus, and Stegosaurus ruled during the Jurassic.

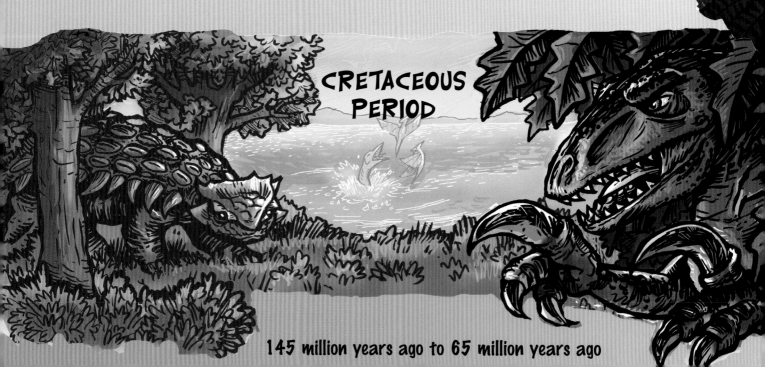

CRETACEOUS PERIOD

145 million years ago to 65 million years ago

Dinosaurs lived during the **Mesozoic Era.** This era is divided into three periods: the **Triassic Period,** the **Jurassic Period,** and the **Cretaceous Period.**

Dinosaurs lived everywhere on Earth. But the Earth looked very different back then!

Even the Rocky Mountains and Badlands, where we live, looked very different than they do today. If you could travel back to the Mesozoic Era in a time machine, this is what you would see:

When: TRIASSIC PERIOD, 240 million years ago to 200 million years ago

Where: Montana, Idaho, Wyoming, North and South Dakota, Utah, and Colorado

What: The Rocky Mountains had not formed yet, and the region was a vast desert!

Who: No dinosaurs lived in our region during the Triassic Period. But they did live in other parts of the world. The continents were all connected back then, forming one giant continent called **Pangaea** *(pan-JEE-uh).*

JURASSIC PERIOD

200 million years ago to 145 million years ago

When: CRETACEOUS PERIOD, 145 million years ago to 65 million years ago

Where: Montana, Idaho, Wyoming, North and South Dakota, Utah, and Colorado

What: The Rocky Mountains formed in the Cretaceous Period! And along eastern Wyoming, Montana, and Colorado was the shore of a large sea!

Who: Ankylosaurus, Deinonychus, Edmontosaurus, Hypacrosaurus, Maiasaura, Tenontosaurus, Thescelosaurus, Triceratops, Tyrannosaurus, Troodon, and Utahraptor roamed during the Cretaceous.

Fossil Hunters

Fantastic Fossil Find

One of the best dinosaur skeletons ever found was discovered by Bob, my field crew chief in Montana. Bob found a very special skeleton of TYRANNOSAURUS REX. It wasn't a new species, or even a **complete skeleton,** but it contained some of the most important scientific information ever found in a dinosaur fossil!

Looking for Bones

When looking for fossils, we just start walking and looking around. Bob went off in one direction, and I went in another. We spread out to cover more land.

Bob climbed up on a high ledge to have his lunch. After he ate his sandwich, he turned around and looked at the big cliff behind him. Sticking out of the cliff was a patch of white bone!

Tyrannosaurus vertebrae and a Global Positioning System (GPS) unit

Bob couldn't reach the bone. It was too high! He stacked up some rocks and climbed on top of them, but he still couldn't reach the bone.

So he walked all the way back to camp and got a chair. He balanced the chair on the stack of rocks and got a close-up look at the bone. It was a foot bone—called a **metatarsal** (MET-uh-TAR-suhl)— from a TYRANNOSAURUS REX!

WHERE'RE THE BONES?

Paleontologists don't just look anywhere for dinosaur fossils. They choose areas where there is SEDIMENTARY ROCK of certain ages. This is where most fossils are preserved. Sedimentary rock is layered. Look out the window when you are riding in the car on the highway. See where the hillside is cut and the rocks are layered? That's sedimentary rock. Other places to find sedimentary rock are cliffs, badlands, and river canyons.

Sedimentary rock

Kinds of Fossils

There are two different kinds of fossils:

- **fossilized body parts** (bones, teeth, claws, and eggs). These are the most commonly found fossils.

- **fossilized impressions or traces** (footprints, teeth marks, skin impressions, nests and burrows, and dung—dinosaur poop!)

Fossilized dinosaur poop is called **COPROLITES** *(KAHP-roh-lites)*. Paleontologists study coprolites to learn about a dinosaur's diet.

Hadrosaur tibia fossil

Fossil duckbill eggs

Fossil Process

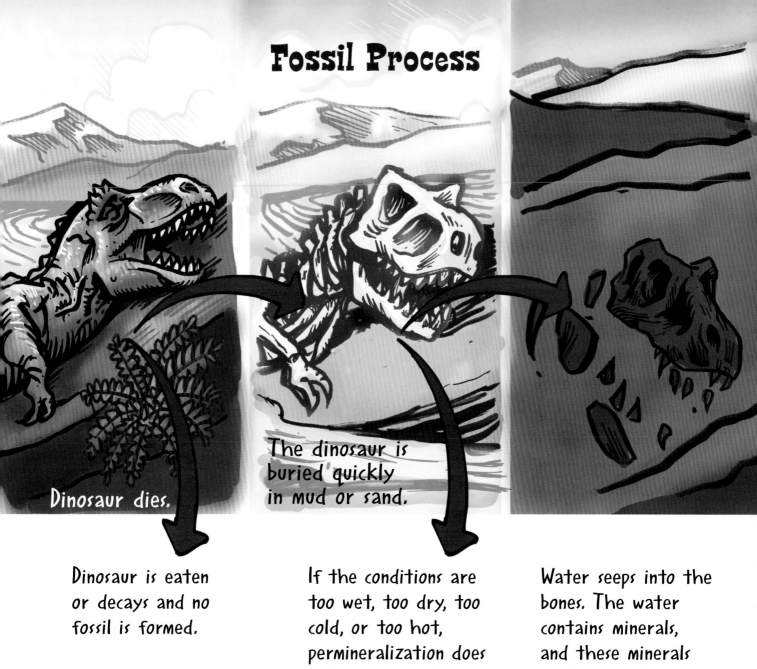

Dinosaur dies.

The dinosaur is buried quickly in mud or sand.

Dinosaur is eaten or decays and no fossil is formed.

If the conditions are too wet, too dry, too cold, or too hot, permineralization does not occur, and the dinosaur decays and no fossil is formed.

Water seeps into the bones. The water contains minerals, and these minerals settle into the spaces in the bones.

JUST THE FACTS!

Most dinosaurs that died did not become fossils. Their bodies decayed and disappeared forever. There are many kinds of dinosaurs that we'll never know about because there is no fossil record of them. The fossil record is all of the fossils that have ever been found.

Old as Dirt

Paleontologists look at a **geological** *(JEE-uh-LOJ-ih-cuhl)* **map** to figure out how old the rocks are in different areas.

We find fossils of dinosaurs in North and South Dakota, Montana, Wyoming, Idaho, Utah, and Colorado because the rocks are the right age.

Dinosaur fossils are very rare in Washington or Oregon because these states are mostly made of rocks that are younger and came from volcanoes.

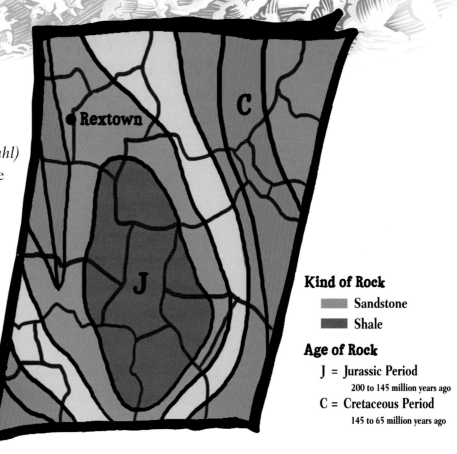

Kind of Rock

Sandstone

Shale

Age of Rock

J = Jurassic Period
200 to 145 million years ago

C = Cretaceous Period
145 to 65 million years ago

WHERE CAN YOU FIND FOSSILS?

Dinosaurs lived everywhere on Earth, but you won't find fossils everywhere. Fossils are only found in rocks of a certain age. Remember, dinosaurs lived from between 240 million years ago to 65 million years ago—a period of time called the MESOZOIC ERA. And certain kinds of dinosaurs lived only at certain periods of time. So to find a particular kind of dinosaur, you have to find rocks from that time.

Look Around

Once you find rock that is the right age, look for areas where rain and wind are eroding the dirt and rocks. Bushes and trees prevent erosion, so you want to go where there aren't any bushes and trees.

Then you have to walk around looking down at the ground. The fossils will be sticking out of the rock just like they were when Bob, my field chief, found the famous TYRANNOSAURUS REX foot bone in Montana.

Hunting for Bones

That's what I do as a paleontologist. No matter where I am in the world, I do the same thing:

- figure out what kind of dinosaur I'm interested in finding

- look at a geological map for the age of rock that dinosaur is found in

- go to the place on the map

Then I walk around, looking down at the ground, searching for any sign of a fossil bone sticking out of the rock.

You don't just go out with a shovel and start digging a hole. You actually have to find the bone first, then you can start digging.

Can You Dig It?

Once my field crew chief realized that the fossil poking out of the cliff was a **TYRANNOSAURUS REX** (**T. REX**) foot bone, we needed to remove and study it.

Bones in Stones

It's very important to remove fossils without damaging them. Using a rock-hammer and a chisel, Bob carefully chipped away at the sandstone that held the T. REX foot bone.

Just One Bone or the Whole Skeleton?

Suddenly, Bob noticed more T. REX bones in the cliff. My general rule about dinosaurs is that if there are three bones in one place that look to

Paleontologists use many special tools to dig up dinosaur fossils.

pick

jackhammer

shovel

rock-hammer

chisel

dental tools

small broom

belong to one animal, then there may be a good skeleton.

It is hard to tell if a few bones are part of a skeleton, or if they are just a few bones that may have washed down an ancient river.

The only way to know for sure was to start digging!

Using jackhammers

Know Your Rocks

These bones were under a massive cliff of sandstone more than 50 feet high. That's as tall as a 5-story building!

To excavate these bones would take lots of people with jackhammers, picks, and shovels and a lot of time!

We needed to figure out if the sedimentary rock where we found the fossil was from the

Students at the quarry

time period when dinosaurs lived. So, we asked a friend for help—a geologist.

A **geologist** (jee-AHL-uh-just) is someone who studies the structure and processes of the Earth. We asked a geologist to look at the rocks that the T. REX bones were in. He said that the rocks were sediments laid down by a river that flowed there about **68 million years ago!**

I knew that old river beds from this time period are great places to find dinosaur skeletons, so we started to dig!

Digging Up Dinosaurs Takes Dino-Might

Students came to the T. REX site and chopped off thousands of pounds of sandstone using jackhammers.

When they got closer to the bones,

skull

vertebra

pelvis

jaw

rib

femur

tibia

T. rex

they switched to smaller digging tools, such as rock-hammers and chisels, so they wouldn't damage the fossils. When they got even closer, they used small paintbrushes and the tools dentists use to fix teeth!

After another week of slow digging, they very carefully removed the last bit of sandstone and found something! The hind legs of the T. REX!

The bones were scattered around, probably disturbed by the ancient river millions of years ago.

We found two thigh bones (femurs, FEE-mers) and a shin bone (tibia, TIH-bee-uh). We also found part of a spine bone (vertebra, VER-teh-bruh), two ribs, and part of an upper jaw.

Mapping a dig site

Fossil Bed Investigation

Glue It!

The first thing paleontologists do after they uncover a fossil is cover it with a very thin glue that soaks in and keeps it from crumbling.

Drawing the map

A finished map showing the positions of the bones

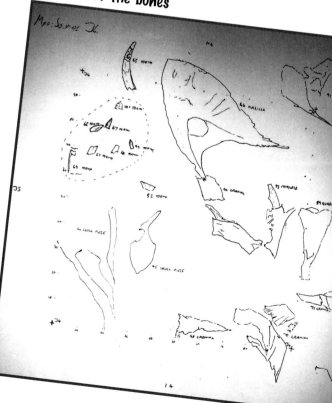

Map It!

Then paleontologists record as much scientific information about the bones as they can. They map the positions of the bones (or pieces of bones) so that when the bones are back at the museum, they can more easily figure out which ones go together—and find out if they all belong to the same animal.

Note It!

If paleontologists aren't careful, they can end up with the bones of two or three different animals. If you put those all together, it might be a cool looking animal, but it would not be good science.

Good science is about being very careful and taking really good notes. Paleontologists, like other scientists, take a lot of measurements and make a lot of notes about all sorts of things.

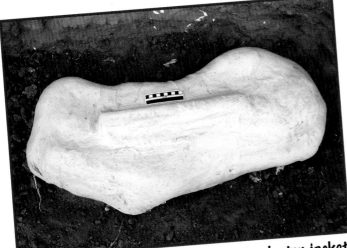

T. rex bone in plaster jacket

Wrap It!

After examining and mapping the fossils, the paleontologist wraps them in wet paper towels and covers them with cloth that has been dipped in plaster of paris. The paper towels keep the plaster from getting on the bones, and the plaster-soaked cloth or burlap is used to hold the bones together. When the plaster jacket hardens, it is rolled over, and then the bottom side is covered with more plaster so that the bone is completely encased and well protected.

The paleontologist then writes on the plaster jacket with a pen. They write lots of information on it so that when the plaster jacket is back in the museum, people will know what it is and where it came from. The plaster-encased bone is then put on a truck and carried off to the museum.

Writing on the jacket

Tools at a dig site

Don't Forget Your Jacket!

Once the bones were exposed, my students placed a plaster-of-paris jacket around the leg bones to protect them.

These jackets protect the bones so we can remove them from the ground all at once without damaging them.

Later, we removed the jacket at the museum and slowly and carefully removed each fossil.

The jackets were so big, we had to use a helicopter to lift them!

DID YOU KNOW?

Ever wonder how paleontologists put a jacket on a fossil? Here's what they do:

- mix up a batch of plaster of paris in a container.
- dip a strip of burlap into the plaster until the strip is completely coated.
- place the strip onto the fossil and the rock around it.
- repeat this over and over until a thick layer of hardened plaster of paris surrounds the fossil. Sometimes pieces of wood are added to make the jacket more stable.

It's a Bird, It's a Plane, It's a...T. rex?

With the extra weight of the plaster of paris, the bones were too heavy for even the helicopter to lift!

We decided to cut one femur into two parts.

It worked! The helicopter carried the T. REX bones through the Montana sky to a truck, which transported them to the museum.

It's Good to Share

When we cut the T. REX bones in two, we sent some of the pieces from the *inside* of the femur to my friend Mary, another paleontologist. I'll explain later why we did this, and I'll tell you about the very important discovery Mary made when she examined the bits of T. REX bone.

STAY TUNED!

DINO-WHEEL

When we don't have a friend with a helicopter, and we are far away from a road, my field crew uses a contraption we invented called a "dino-wheel." A dino-wheel has a motorcycle wheel in the middle and a set of handlebars on each side. One person pulls the front handle-bars, and another person pushes the back handlebars. With the dino-wheel, two people can move plaster jackets weighing several hundred pounds!

Dino-wheel

MAKE YOUR OWN TOOLKIT

The next time you visit your dentist, ask if they'll give you their old (and clean) dental picks. Then get yourself a little paintbrush, a small whisk broom, some glue, and an ice pick, and you will have the tools we use to carefully expose a dinosaur fossil.

BUT REMEMBER: you cannot dig for fossils without permission. Join one of the dig programs listed on page 47—and bring your toolkit!

Tons of Rock

With the leg bones removed, the students kept digging, looking for the skull, pelvis, and more ribs and vertebrae. They dug up more than 2,000 tons of rock! That's enough rock to fill 50 dump trucks!

Again, as the crew got closer to the bones, they again used smaller tools so they wouldn't accidentally damage a fossil.

Suddenly, they found the skull, the missing shin bone, and several other parts of the skeleton!

IT'S THE LAW!

You can't just go anywhere and start digging up fossils. Every piece of land is owned by somebody, so you have to get permission if you want to explore and look for fossils. IT IS ILLEGAL TO DIG UP OR TAKE FOSSILS FROM FEDERAL OR STATE LAND! Remember, looking for fossils is NOT souvenir hunting. Fossils are critical for research and give us important information about the history of the planet!

Missing Bones

The students did not find many of the vertebrae or the pelvis.

T. rex excavation

These bones must have weathered out of the cliff over the last few thousands of years, or maybe they had washed down that ancient river **68 million years ago.** We will never know.

Very Important Dinosaur

Even though the T. REX skeleton wasn't a complete skeleton, it is still a very important specimen because of its size and its preservation.

In fact, this T. REX skeleton is the **most well-preserved dinosaur skeleton ever found in the world!**

Later, I'll tell you why this is important!

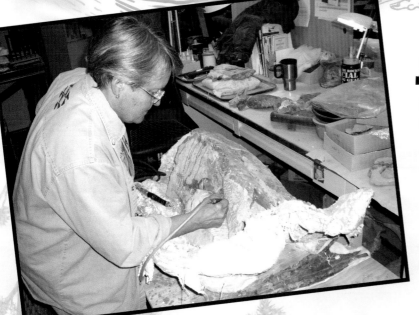
Getting the fossil out

A Prehistoric Puzzle: Putting Dinosaurs Back Together

Jackets Off!

When the plaster jackets arrive at the museum, a **preparator** *(pruh-PAIR-uh-ter,* a person whose job it is to remove the fossils from the jackets) opens them using a cast cutter. A cast cutter is a machine that doctors use to cut casts off people who have broken their legs or arms.

Detail Work

Preparators use tools like dental picks and even small jackhammers. Tool preparators also use sandblasters to shoot fine dust at the rock-coated bone and wear away the rock, but not the bone.

When the preparator gets to the bone, a very thin glue is soaked into the bone so that it does not break apart.

Preparators have to have lots of patience—their jobs can take months, sometimes even years! Fossil preparation is a very slow process!

Sandblasting

Casts and Molds

Once the bones are removed, they are given a museum number and put into the museum collection to be studied.

Sometimes, special bones are duplicated so that other scientists can study them without having to remove the real bone from the museum.

To make a duplicate, or a **cast,** a **mold** has to be made. The real bone is coated with liquid rubber that becomes flexible rubber when it dries.

The fossil is removed from the mold. The space where the fossil was is then filled with plaster of paris or plastic resin. When the plaster or plastic hardens, it is taken out of the mold and painted to look like the original bone. Most dinosaur skeletons that you see in museums are not actually fossils. They are plaster or plastic casts of the original fossils.

We do this because putting together and displaying (mounting) real dinosaur fossils is not good for them. If a plaster or plastic skeleton falls down, it's okay because we can make another one, but if the real skeleton gets damaged, it can't be replaced.

T. rex teeth

Fossil

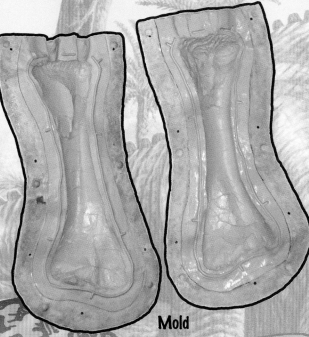

Mold

Cast

How to make your own cast of a "fossil":

modeling clay

paintbrush

seashell

plaster of paris

petroleum jelly

What you need:
- ✓ modeling clay
- ✓ a chicken bone or a seashell
- ✓ petroleum jelly or castor oil
- ✓ a small paintbrush
- ✓ plaster of paris

How to make a mold:
① Knead the clay
② Flatten it until it is 3/4 inch thick
③ Brush the petroleum jelly or castor oil on the shell or bone
④ Press the shell or bone into the clay
⑤ Remove the shell or bone

How to make a cast:
① Mix the plaster of paris, following the instructions on the package
② Pour the plaster into the mold
③ When the plaster is hardened, remove it from the mold

This plaster cast is a replica of the original shell or bone!

What Do Fossils Tell Us?

Paleontologists learn many secrets about dinosaurs by studying fossil bones and trace fossils.

Bone Science

Most paleontologists examine the shapes of the bones and compare the bones of one animal to the bones of others to try to figure out what kind of animal it was.

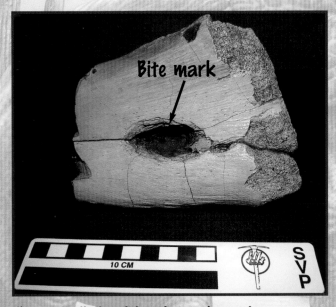

Bite mark

10 CM

SVP

This duckbill ulna (elbow) bone has a large T. REX bite mark. From the bite marks and tooth punctures found in other fossils, we know that T. REX ate TRICERATOPS, the duckbilled EDMONTOSAURUS, and even other TYRANNOSAURUS.

An Unhappy Meal?

Paleontologists study dinosaur teeth, too. Once they've figured out what a dinosaur's teeth look like, they can figure out what it eats.

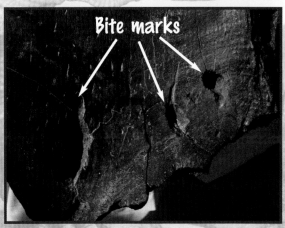

Bite marks

T. REX teeth made these holes in the pelvis of a TRICERATOPS. Therefore we know that T. REXES ate TRICERATOPS.

Tricky Trackway

Paleontologists also study **trackways** to learn about how an animal moved. Utah and Colorado are good places to find dinosaur footprints and trackways.

Identifying footprints can be tricky because tracks look different in different kinds of mud. If the mud is really thick, an animal sinks in further and creates a footprint that looks different than it would in drier or thinner mud.

Trackways are also tricky because when there are many footprints together, it's hard to figure out if several dinosaurs were walking together—in a herd—or if they walked through the same area at different times.

TAPHONOMY

(taff-AHN-oh-mee) is the study of what happened to an animal after it died, decayed, and was fossilized or otherwise preserved. Among many other things, this information can help determine what kind of an environment the dinosaur lived in.

Brachiosaurus herd

Other Clues

By examining the rocks where dinosaur skeletons are found, paleontologists can figure out what the dinosaurs' environment was like. Did they live in a swamp? A desert? A jungle? The fossils of plants and other kinds of animals also give us clues about their environment.

If we find coal with the fossil, that means the environment was once a swamp.

If we find traces of ancient palm trees, then we know that the area was a subtropical environment—like Louisiana or Florida today.

Studying the Tyrannosaurus rex

When the T. REX specimen we found was ready for study, I examined the skull first. I measured its teeth, examined its cheekbones, and peered into the space where its brain had been.

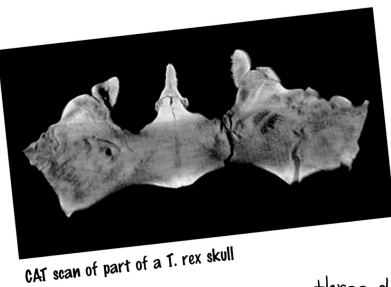

CAT scan of part of a T. rex skull

I measured the teeth with a tool called **calipers** (KAL-ih-perz). To study the cheekbones, I used a **microscope.** And to look inside the cavity where the brain had been, I used a **CAT scanner.** A CAT scanner takes x-rays and then uses them to create a three-dimensional picture.

Because I don't have a CAT scanner, I took the brain case of the T. REX up to the hospital!

We looked at the CAT scan pictures and examined the space in the skull where the brain once was. We measured the space and compared it to the brain sizes of other animals.

No Brainiac

This T. REX was a big dinosaur, but it had a brain about the size of a sheep's brain. Even sheep are more intelligent than T. REXES were. A T. REX was probably about as smart as a duck—which is to say that T. REXES weren't very smart.

But if you're 30 feet long, weigh 8,000 pounds, and have a mouth full of banana-size teeth, you probably don't have to be very smart!

Look Inside

Besides studying the shape of bones and comparing them to the bones of other dinosaurs, we also look inside the bone tissues, too. This can tell us how old the dinosaur was when it died, whether it was warm-blooded or cold-blooded, or even how fast it grew up. We figure this stuff out by using a microscope and looking at the bone's structure.

The study of the inside of bones is called **bone histology** (bone his-TAHL-uh-gee).

CHECK OUT THOSE CHOPS!

Dinosaurs continually lost and grew new teeth, getting new ones every year. Humans have baby teeth, and as we grow older they fall out and are replaced with our adult teeth. That means that we replace our teeth once during our life. Dinosaurs replaced their teeth EVERY YEAR, so that means that they probably never got cavities or had a toothache! Anytime they broke or lost a tooth, they just grew a new one.

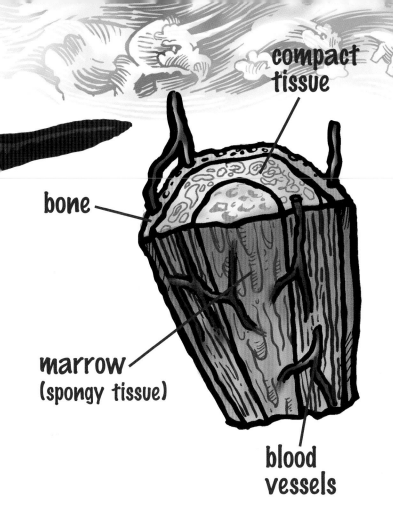

compact
tissue

bone

marrow
(spongy tissue)

blood
vessels

Bones and Blood

If you break a chicken bone in two and look inside, you will see some spongy tissue called **marrow** *(MAIR-oh).* You will also see that part of the bone is very dense and compact. This compact part has holes in it that held blood vessels when the animal was alive. The more blood vessels that the bone has, the faster the bone grew. The fewer the blood vessels, the slower the bone grew.

Ring Around the Dinosaur

Dinosaurs grew faster than reptiles do today. Small Orodromeus grew slowly, while huge Brachiosaurus grew quickly.

Paleontologists sometimes find faint lines inside bones—similar to the rings inside of a tree. The rings inside a tree represent times when the tree's growth slowed down or stopped. Each ring represents a year, so if you want to know the age of a tree, you count its rings. The same goes for most animal bones. Inside many mammal bones, all reptile bones, and dinosaur and ancient bird bones are the same kinds of lines or rings. And, like trees, each line represents one year.

T. rex bone rings

Secrets of the Bones

T. rex Teenager

We counted the lines in the T. REX bones and discovered it was 18 years old!

The two oldest T. REX specimens that we know of are the T. REX known as Sue (found in South Dakota and displayed in Chicago) and the specimen known as MOR 008 at the Museum of the Rockies in Montana. Both of these dinosaurs were around 25 years old when they died. We don't know if 25 is young or old for a T. REX because we don't know how long they lived. We can only tell the ages of the ones we find, and so far there are only about 35 partial TYRANNOSAURUS skeletons in the whole world!

The Big Discovery

The most interesting study of the T. REX fossils was made by my friend Mary. She examined the pieces of bone we had wrapped in tin foil after breaking the femur so that we could lift it with the helicopter.

One of the two oldest T. rex specimens ever found

Big Find, Big Mystery

We learned many things about the T. REX by looking at its marrow and rings, but Mary made the most important discoveries when she looked at the blood vessels inside the bones.

Blood vessels and blood cells

What Mary found were **blood vessels with blood cells inside.** And, the most incredible thing about the blood vessels is that they are still flexible and stretchy! The blood vessels and blood cells had remained preserved for **68 million years!** How the blood vessels stayed flexible is still a mystery, and scientists are working hard to try and figure it out.

T. rex known as Sue, one of the two oldest T. rexes ever found.

IT'S A GIRL!

But, this is still not everything that was found inside the bones of the T. REX. A very special kind of bone called **medullary bone** (MED-yoo-LAIR-ee bone) was found inside the marrow cavity. Before this find, medullary bone was only known to exist in female bird legs.

Medullary bone is loaded with calcium; it's where the animal stores the calcium it uses to make eggs.

Since only female animals make eggs, we knew that this T. REX was a female dinosaur and that she died just before she laid eggs.

This T. REX is only the second dinosaur ever found that we could tell if it was a female or a male! The other dinosaur was an Oviraptor that was found in China; it still had two eggs in its body.

T. rex

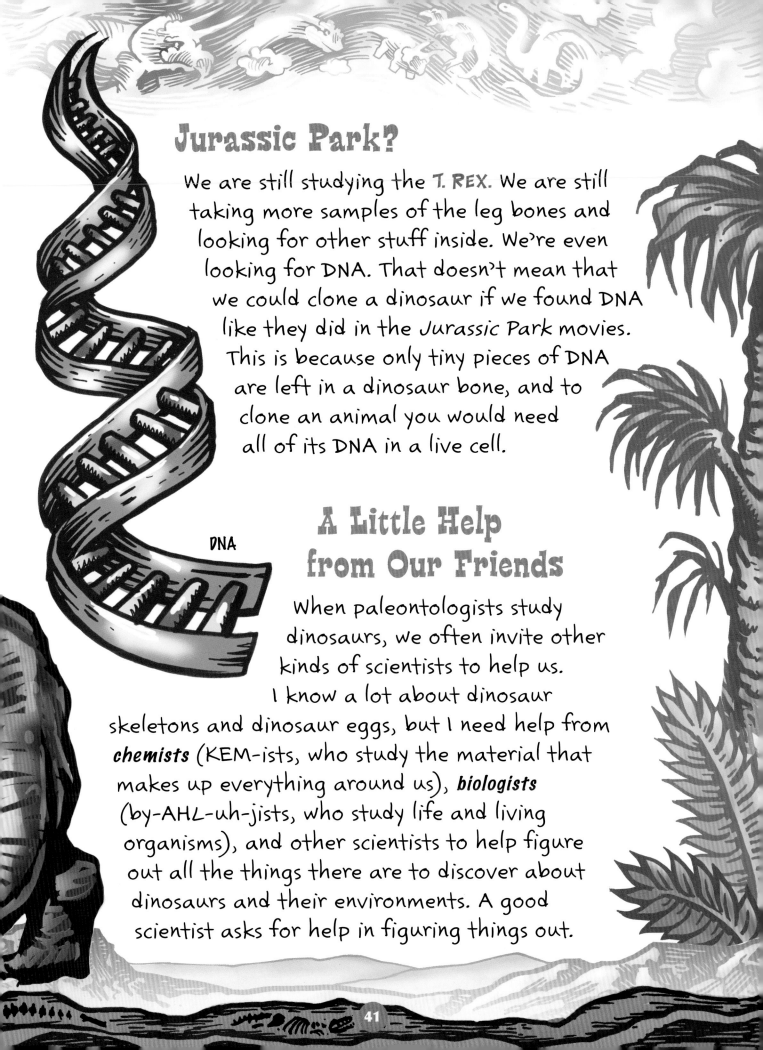

Jurassic Park?

We are still studying the T. REX. We are still taking more samples of the leg bones and looking for other stuff inside. We're even looking for DNA. That doesn't mean that we could clone a dinosaur if we found DNA like they did in the *Jurassic Park* movies. This is because only tiny pieces of DNA are left in a dinosaur bone, and to clone an animal you would need all of its DNA in a live cell.

DNA

A Little Help from Our Friends

When paleontologists study dinosaurs, we often invite other kinds of scientists to help us. I know a lot about dinosaur skeletons and dinosaur eggs, but I need help from *chemists* (KEM-ists, who study the material that makes up everything around us), *biologists* (by-AHL-uh-jists, who study life and living organisms), and other scientists to help figure out all the things there are to discover about dinosaurs and their environments. A good scientist asks for help in figuring things out.

Egg Mountain

There are very few dinosaur sites in the world where you can get as much information about the lives of dinosaurs as we have gotten from the site in Montana that is now called Egg Mountain.

We found a large nest of eggs belonging to a new kind of duckbilled dinosaur called MAIASAURA PEEBLESORUM. We also found the bones of 15 babies—each almost 3 feet long!

From just this one site, which covers an area less than 1 square mile, we discovered two new kinds of dinosaurs and evidence that some dinosaurs traveled in gigantic herds, nested in colonies like birds, and cared for their young like birds.

DID YOU KNOW?

We made many other interesting discoveries at Egg Mountain. We found a gigantic accumulation of adult and juvenile Maiasaura skeletons that apparently died in some kind of catastrophic event such as a volcanic eruption. We found the remains of more than 10,000 skeletons. It's the largest accumulation of dinosaur bones found anywhere on earth!

Cleveland-Lloyd Quarry

In one place in Utah, called the Cleveland-Lloyd Quarry, more than 10,000 bones have been dug up! These bones represent dinosaurs like **CAMARASAURUS**, **STEGOSAURUS**, **CAMPTOSAURUS**, and **ALLOSAURUS**. The most interesting thing about this quarry is that most of the bones belong to **ALLOSAURUS**. And some people have concluded that this large number of bones means that **ALLOSAURUS** hunted in groups or packs.

I think all dinosaurs lived in some kind of a group. Some groups were family groups and some groups were herds, and some may well have been packs. I think dinosaurs were very social, meaning that they didn't often live by themselves. Most birds are pretty social as well.

Maiasaura peeblesorum

Egg
Mountain

MONTANA

IDAHO

WYOMING

Great
Salt Lake

UTAH

Dinosaur
National
Monument

Cleveland-
Lloyd
Dinosaur
Quarry

COLORADO

NORTH DAKOTA

SOUTH DAKOTA

Missouri River

These are just a few of the dinosaurs that once lived in this region.

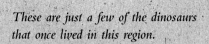

ALLOSAURUS—JURASSIC PERIOD

Allosaurus was a large, meat-eating dinosaur that killed sauropods by slashing them with its blade-shaped teeth.

ANKYLOSAURUS—CRETACEOUS PERIOD

Ankylosaurus was a large, armored, plant-eating dinosaur that used the large club on its tail for defense.

BRACHIOSAURUS—JURASSIC PERIOD

Brachiosaurus was one of the largest dinosaurs. It fed on the tops of giant conifer trees and tree ferns.

DEINONYCHUS—CRETACEOUS PERIOD

Deinonychus had hollow bones, like today's birds.

TENONTOSAURUS—CRETACEOUS PERIOD

Tenontosaurus was a medium-sized plant-eater that had a very long, rigid tail.

DIPLODOCUS—JURASSIC PERIOD

A full-grown *Diplodocus* was more than 80 feet long, but its head was only 2 feet long and its brain was the size of a person's fist.

EDMONTOSAURUS—CRETACEOUS PERIOD

Edmontosaurus was the largest of the duck-billed dinosaurs. It grew to more than 50 feet in length, larger than a Tyrannosaurus.

HYPACROSAURUS—CRETACEOUS PERIOD

Hypacrosaurus was one of the crested duck-billed dinosaurs that used its head crest to make honking sounds.

MAIASAURA—CRETACEOUS PERIOD

Maiasaura was a plant-eating dinosaur that cared for its babies by bringing food to them in the nest.

STEGOSAURUS—JURASSIC PERIOD

Stegosaurus was a plant-eating dinosaur that used the large plates on its back to show off and scare away meat-eaters.

TRICERATOPS—CRETACEOUS PERIOD

Triceratops was a plant-eating, horned dinosaur whose horns changed shape and direction as it grew into an adult.

TROODON—CRETACEOUS PERIOD

Troodon was a medium-sized predatory dinosaur that probably climbed up on its prey to make a kill.

TYRANNOSAURUS—CRETACEOUS PERIOD

Tyrannosaurus adults had bone-crushing teeth that they used for scavenging dead animals.

UTAHRAPTOR—CRETACEOUS PERIOD

Utahraptor was one of the largest predatory dinosaurs. It most likely used its killing claws to rip open the bodies of its prey.

WHAT'S IN A NAME ?

To name a new kind of plant or animal, including a dinosaur, there are certain rules that a person has to follow. The name can be from any language, but it has to be turned into Latin. You take the name you chose and add either "saura" or "saurus" to it. "Saura" is for female names, and "saurus" is for male names. If a dinosaur were named after me, it would be "Jackosaurus." If it were named after my friend Mary, her dinosaur name would be "Maryosaura."

IF YOU HAD A DINOSAUR NAMED AFTER YOU, WHAT WOULD IT BE CALLED?

Dinosaur National Monument

In most places where dinosaurs lived, we can find lots of skeletons, but there isn't enough information to be able to figure out much about how they lived. For example, in some states paleontologists find huge accumulations of skeletons, like those at Dinosaur National Monument in Utah and Colorado, but these dinosaurs probably floated down a river and piled up against fallen trees or on sandbars. These are good spots to collect lots of different kinds of dinosaurs, but not to figure out life stories. At Dinosaur National Monument, the dinosaurs are all from the Jurassic Period. There are many different kinds of SAUROPODS (dinosaurs that used to be called "BRONTOSAURS"), and STEGOSAURUS and the meat-eaters ALLOSAURUS and CERATOSAURUS.

Stegosaurus

See the Bones

Beneath your feet are the bones of some of the most amazing creatures to ever walk the Earth. Now that you've traveled back in time to see where they lived, hunted fossils in the sedimentary rock, and learned the secrets of the bones, it's your turn to discover!

The best museums use fossils to tell stories about the incredible lives of dinosaurs. Here are some good programs in our area:

Colorado
Dinosaur Journey Museum
Museum of Western Colorado
888-488-DINO
www.dinodigs.org
minimum age: 5 (must be accompanied by an adult)

Montana
Judith River Dinosaur Institute
406-654-2323
nmurphy@ttc-cmc.net
www.montanadinosaurdigs.com
minimum age: 14

Makoshika Dinosaur Museum
406-377-1637
www.makoshika.com
www.paleokids.com
minimum age: 6 (must be accompanied by an adult)

Museum of the Rockies
406-994-DINO (3466)
www.mor@montana.edu
www.montana.edu/wwwmor/
no minimum age

Timescale Adventures
800-238-6873
406-469-2211
info@timescale.org
www.timescale.org
no minimum age

North Dakota
Marmarth Research Foundation
610-937-7916
612-382-8978
www.marmarthresearchfound.org
minimum age: 14 (must be accompanied by an adult)

Pioneer Trails Regional Museum
701-523-3600
ptrm@ptrm.org
www.ptrm.org
kids under 18 must be accompanied by an adult

South Dakota
South Dakota School of Mines and
Technology, Museum of Geology
800-544-8162, extension 2467
kids under 18 must be accompanied by an adult

Utah
College of Eastern Utah Prehistoric Museum
UFOP Dinosaur Digs
http://museum.ceu.edu
minimum age: 12

Wyoming
The Wyoming Dinosaur Center
800-455-DINO
307-864-2997
wdinoc@wyodino.org
www.wyodino.org
minimum age: 8

Glossary-saurus

ANKYLOSAURS — armored dinosaurs with tail clubs (such as *Ankylosaurus*)

AVIAN DINOSAURS – birds

BIOLOGY – the study of living organisms

BONE HISTOLOGY – the study of the internal structures of bone

CAUDAL VERTEBRAE – the bones of the spine that make up the tail

CERATOPSIANS – horned dinosaurs (such as *Triceratops*)

CERVICAL VERTEBRAE – the bones of the spine that make up the neck

CLADISTICS – a method of determining which living organisms are most closely related to one another

CURATOR – a person who identifies and cares for fossil remains in a museum

DINOSAURS – reptiles that walked with their legs directly under their bodies, not sprawled out to the sides

DORSAL VERTEBRAE – the bones of the spine that the ribs attach to

DROMAEOSAURS – meat-eating dinosaurs with a sickle claw on each hind foot (these are the dinosaurs often called "raptors")

EVOLUTION – the idea that all living organisms are related to one another and that living organisms change to adapt to their environment

FEMUR – the hind leg bone that runs from the pelvis to the knee (the femur is often called the thigh bone)

FIBULA – the smaller of the lower hind leg bones that connect the knee and ankle

FORMATION – a sedimentary rock unit that covers a large area and is of a certain geological age

GEOLOGY – the study of the Earth and the rocks it is made of

HADROSAURS – duck-billed dinosaurs (such as *Maiasaura*)

HUMERUS – the front leg bone that fits into the shoulder blade (scapula) and runs from the shoulder to the elbow

HYPSILOPHODONTID – many of the little primitive plant-eating dinosaurs that walked on two legs (such as *Orodromeus*)

ILIUM – the bone of the pelvis that attaches to the sacrum

INVERTEBRATES – animals lacking bony skeletons

ISCHIUM – the bone of the pelvis that extends down and backward from the ilium

NODOSAURS – armored dinosaurs with no tail club (such as *Sauropelta*)

NON-AVIAN DINOSAURS – the dinosaurs that do not include birds

ORNITHISCHIANS – all of the dinosaurs that are more closely related to *Triceratops* than they are related to birds

ORNITHOMIMIDS – the ostrich-like dinosaurs

PALEONTOLOGY – the study of life in past geologic time

PREPARATORY – a person who cleans the rock off fossils

PROTOCERATOPSIANS – the closest ancestors of the horned dinosaurs (such as *Protoceratops*)

PUBIS – the bone of the pelvis that points down and forward from the ilium

RADIUS – the smaller of the lower front leg bones that run from the elbow to the wrist

REPTILES – animals that lay eggs on land but are not related to mammals or mammal relatives

SACRUM – the bones of the spine to which the pelvic bones attach

SAURISCHIANS – all of the dinosaurs that are more closely related to living birds than to ornithischian dinosaurs

SAUROPODS – long-necked dinosaurs (such as *Brachiosaurus*)

SCAPULA – the shoulder blade

STERNAL – the bones to which the sternum (the bone at the center of the chest) is attached

STRATA – a single layer of sedimentary rock

TAPHONOMY – the study of how animals die and get covered up with sediment

THEROPODS – meat-eating saurischian dinosaurs that walked on two legs (such as *Tyrannosaurus rex*)

TIBIA – the larger of the lower hind leg bones that run from the ankle to the knee, connecting with the femur at the knee (the tibia is sometimes called the shin bone)

TYRANNOSAURS – meat-eating theropods that had very short arms and two-fingered hands

ULNA – the front leg bone that, with the smaller radius bone, runs from the wrist to the elbow, joining with the humerus at the elbow

VERTEBRA – the bones that form the spine and protect the spinal cord

VERTEBRATES – animals with bony skeletons